The Amish

Why They Enchant Us

DONALD B. KRAYBILL

Herald
Press

Scottdale, Pennsylvania
Waterloo, Ontario

Library of Congress Cataloging-in-Publication Data

Kraybill, Donald B.
    The Amish : why they enchant us / Donald B. Kraybill.
        p. cm.
Includes bibliographical references.
    ISBN 0-8361-9241-9 (pbk. : alk. paper)
    1. Amish.   I. Title.
    BX8129.A5 .K73 2003
    289.7'3—dc21

                                                            2002153427

Photo and graphic credits: Linda Eberly: 7, 25; Dennis Hughes: front cover, 5, 12, 15, 22, 27, 31 (bottom), 34, 35, 37, 41, 43, 46; Lucian Niemeyer: 20, 23; Daniel Rodriguez: 14, 33, 36, 44; Blair Seitz: 11, 24, 40; Shirley Wenger: 39; Doyle Yoder: 1, 3, 6, 8, 9, 19, 26, 28, 31 (top), 42, back cover.

All author royalties from this book are contributed to a nonprofit foundation for distribution to charitable causes.

THE AMISH: WHY THEY ENCHANT US
Copyright © 2003 by Herald Press, Scottdale, Pa. 15683
        Published simultaneously in Canada by Herald Press,
        Waterloo, Ont. N2L 6H7. All rights reserved
Library of Congress Catalog Card Number: 2002153427
International Standard Book Number: 0-8361-9241-9
Printed in the United States of America
Book and cover design by Beth Oberholtzer

10 09 08 07 06 05 04 03   10 9 8 7 6 5 4 3 2 1

To order or request information, please call
1-800-759-4447 (individuals); 1-800-245-7894 (trade).
Website: www.mph.org

Why the Amish Enchant Us

The Amish are one of North America's more fascinating religious communities. Still speaking a German or Swiss dialect, they have created their own cultural world in the midst of contemporary society. They have stubbornly refused to be swallowed up by American culture, but they are not social antiques frozen in time. They are a dynamic and flourishing community. What are the secrets of their success? What is their source of wisdom? And why do they enchant us?

We are likely drawn to the Amish for many reasons: their sense of place, their social stability, and their stubborn resistance to modern

Although many Amish are involved in small businesses they remain a rural people and much of their recreation is informal and related to nature. These children enjoy a dip in a nearby stream.

culture. Amid the stress and press of contemporary life, we are intrigued by their stable communities and strong social bonds. Their robust families and slower pace of life also lure us. We are amazed that they are happy without televisions, computers, and high-speed cars. Perhaps our enchantment with the Amish also belies our discontent with modern life. We may not always agree with them, but we admire their courage to practice their faith in the face of high-tech life.

Amish people may look quaint at first glance, but upon closer inspection, we discover that some of their values challenge our cherished views. We dislike their conformity to plain dress and their limits on technology. Moreover, we are troubled by a people that reject not only college, but even high school and the study of science. Indeed, many Amish practices fly in the face of prized virtues like diversity, choice, progress, and global awareness. Thus, ironically, we find ourselves drawn to a people who spurn some of the cardinal values of modern life.

We are enchanted by a community that has found a way to preserve a strong sense of meaning, identity, and belonging—values that are often trampled afoot by the hyper pace of high-tech living. Yet, many people crave these very values that the Amish embody. What can we learn from our Amish neighbors who have crafted such a different world within the modern mosaic?

Growth and Diversity

We might expect a traditional group that rejects higher education and computer technology to be dying. Surprisingly, the Amish are growing. Indeed their numbers double about every twenty years. Counting adults and children, they number nearly 200,000 souls. One Amish woman, joked, "If we keep growing so fast, soon half the world will be Amish and the other half will be taxi drivers who haul us around." How do they manage to flourish in the midst of modern life?

The diversity of Amish communities is reflected in the color of their carriages. Local church affiliations specify the color and style of carriages. Colors include yellow, white, tan, black, and gray. Some carriages are made from wood, others from fiberglass, and in some communities they are constructed from plastic. The Amish call them buggies.

Large families and strong retention rates propel Amish growth. On the average, families have about seven children, but it's not unusual to have ten or more. Typically, about 85 percent of their youth join the church. But, in some communities, more than 95 percent join. Although the Amish do not seek converts, outsiders may join if they comply with Amish guidelines. Several dozen "English," as outsiders are called, have entered their flock in recent decades.

The Amish reside in more than 200 communities in about twenty-five states, mostly east of the Mississippi. Some also live in the Canadian province of Ontario. The three most populous states are Ohio, Pennsylvania, and Indiana. New communities form yearly, while others flounder and die. The largest community in Holmes County, Ohio, claims nearly 200 Amish congregations. Small communities may have only one or two congregations, which the Amish call a church district. The Amish have more than 1,400 local church districts across the country.

Four groups carry the Amish name: Beachy Amish, Amish Mennonites, New Order Amish, and Old Order Amish. The Beachy Amish and Amish Mennonites own automobiles and use public utility electricity. This book focuses on Old Order and New Order Amish groups that use horse-and-buggy transportation. The New Order groups make up less than 10 percent of the horse-and-buggy-driving Amish of North America. Compared to Old Order groups, New Order churches, among other things, permit greater use of technology, encourage more personal Bible study, and have stricter guidelines for their youth.

At first glance, the Amish look alike, but there are, in fact, more than a dozen different subgroups. Each has its own practices. Some have black top buggies, while other groups sport yellow, gray, or white tops. Even within subgroups, diversity abounds. Some congregations permit the use of power lawn mowers, but others do not.

Many elderly Amish live in a Grossdawdy (grandparent) house or apartment adjacent to the homes of one of their adult children. Grandparents continue to live useful lives helping with chores, interacting with their grandchildren, and visiting with neighbors and relatives.

Note: Districts in Idaho, Maine, and Washington = 1; Montana = 4.
SOURCE: *Raber's Almanac* (2003), *Anabaptist World USA* (2001) and informants.

Distribution of Old Order and New Order Amish Congregations in North America. The majority are in Ohio, Pennsylvania, and Indiana.

The farmers in one church district may milk their cows by hand while their neighbors use automatic milkers. Some communities are wealthy and others are rather poor. But despite their differences today, the Amish share a common history.

Origins and Beliefs

The Amish trace their history to the Anabaptist movement that emerged during the Protestant Reformation in Europe in the 1500s.

7

All Amish communities have specific standards of dress for adult members including hats for men and headgear for women. The styles and colors of Amish dress vary considerably from community to community.

Beginning in Switzerland in 1525, and spreading to other regions of Europe, the Anabaptists refused to baptize babies. They argued that only adults who had voluntarily decided to follow Christ should be baptized. Their defiant acts were a capital crime in a world that expected all babies to be baptized. The young radicals were soon called "Anabaptists," meaning rebaptizers, because they had already been baptized as infants. The Anabaptists sought to practice the teachings of Jesus in daily life and gave greater allegiance to the Bible than to civil government. They were, in fact, some of the earliest proponents of the separation of church and state.

The Anabaptists outraged civil and religious authorities who thought the church and state should be a single social fabric. Severe persecution began in 1527 and continued for many years. Anabaptists were considered heretics and many were executed. They were burned at the stake, drowned in lakes, tortured in public spectacles, and starved in dungeons. A 1200-page book, the *Martyrs Mirror: The Bloody Theater of the Defenseless Christians,* records many stories of their torture. Amish ministers often retell stories from the *Martyrs Mirror* in their sermons today.

The harsh persecution drove many Anabaptists into hiding in rural areas and confirmed their belief that the church should be a separate

Children in most Amish communities are dressed in similar styles to their parents. This father is a member of a traditional community that has more conservative styles of dress and haircuts than many Amish.

community in the larger society. Separation from the world soon became a key tenet of faith for many heirs of the early Anabaptists.

The Amish emerged in 1693 as a distinctive group among the Anabaptists living in Switzerland and in the Alsace region of France. An Anabaptist leader named Jakob Ammann sought to renew church life, but other leaders did not welcome his ideas. Among other changes, Ammann called for shunning wayward members of the church in order to maintain its witness and purity. The differences led to a division in 1693, and Ammann's followers were soon called Amish. Many other Anabaptists eventually took the name Mennonite from a Dutch Anabaptist leader, Menno Simons.

The Amish migrated to the Americas in several waves in the mid-1700s and again in the 1800s. They formed communities in Pennsylvania, Ohio, and Indiana and eventually spread to other states. They often settled near their spiritual cousins, the Mennonites. Today, some Old Order Mennonite groups use horse-and-buggy transportation, but the majority of Mennonites drive cars, wear contemporary clothing, support higher education, and use modern technology. Old Order Mennonites sometimes cooperate with the Amish on schools and publications, but generally the Amish and Mennonites live separately even though they share Anabaptist roots.

Yielding to Others

The core value of Amish society is captured in the German word *Gelassenheit* (Gay-la-sen-hite). Roughly translated, Gelassenheit means yielding oneself to a higher authority. The Amish speak of "giving themselves up" to the church. Gelassenheit carries many meanings—self-surrender, submission, yielding to the will of God and to others, contentment, and a calm spirit. Most important, Gelassenheit is the opposite of a bold individualism that promotes self-interest at every turn. This is the point where Amish society diverges far from contemporary culture.

Work is highly esteemed in Amish culture. Children assume many responsibilities at an early age in shops, on farms, and around homes and gardens. These children are hauling hay bales.

Children are taught the meaning of Gelassenheit in the lines of a schoolroom verse:

> I must be a Christian child
> Gentle, patient, meek, and mild;
> Must be honest, simple, true
> In my words and actions too.
> I must cheerfully obey,
> Giving up my will and way.

The Amish abhor pride and teach the importance of humility. Pride refers to attitudes and actions that clamor for attention and recognition. Showy clothing, wristwatches, fancy drapes, or ornaments on a harness, signal pride in Amish life. The prohibitions against cosmetics, jewelry, and personal photographs are designed to prevent pride. Children are taught that "I" is the middle letter of pride. The motto JOY reminds children that Jesus is first, You are last, and Others are in between.

Humility and obedience are twin virtues in Amish culture. A spirit of humility signals respect for others. Members are taught to obey those with authority over them: children their parents, students their teachers, wives their husbands, members their leaders, and younger ministers their bishop. Everyone is expected to obey the will of God as taught by the community. Despite the strong emphasis on humility and obedience, the Amish express great respect for the dignity of each person.

Community and tradition also play important roles in Amish life. Indeed, the community takes precedence over the individual. The welfare of the community ranks above individual rights and choices. Communal wisdom, accumulated over the decades, is valued more than the opinion of one person. Traditional beliefs and practices are esteemed above scientific findings.

Gelassenheit also shapes the Amish view of salvation. Rather than emphasizing emotional experiences and the assurance of salvation, Amish leaders speak of a "living hope," an abiding belief that

Women are adept at handling horses and driving carriages. Some states require carriages to have licenses. A few conservative Amish groups use reflective tape on their carriages and refuse to use the red triangles. These carriages have both, as well as battery-powered electric lights.

God will grant faithful followers eternal life. Thus, they refrain from the individualistic, evangelical language of "personal" experience and "born again" conversion. In a spirit of humility, they trust in God's providence for their salvation, believing that it flows from obedient living in the community of faith.

Rules for Daily Living

Amish values are translated into guidelines for daily living called the *Ordnung,* a German word that means rules and order. The Ordnung is a set of expectations for daily living. Usually unwritten, the rules are passed on by practice and oral tradition. They are updated as new issues arise. Children learn the rules by observation. Many expectations—the taboos against divorce, television, and military service—need little discussion because they are simply taken for granted. More controversial issues—the use of cell phones, computers, fancy lawn ornaments, or immodest dress—are addressed by leaders in congregational meetings.

Members of each church district affirm the Ordnung twice a year before the spring and fall communion service. The details of the Ordnung vary by subgroup, as well as by local congregation. Some congregations, for example, permit the use of propane gas stoves and refrigerators while others do not. Most Amish homes have indoor bathrooms and plumbing, but members of more conservative groups walk to the outhouse. The Ordnung, said one person, is "an agreement among our members about how we should live." The words of a minister echo this belief, "If members respect the Ordnung, it generates peace, love, contentment, equality, and unity." Nevertheless, disagreements over the details of the Ordnung can at times become quite contentious.

The Ordnung defines expectations and taboos for conduct ranging from personal dress to the use of technology. All Amish groups expect men and women to wear distinctive clothing. Married men are expected to grow a beard and wear an Amish-style hat and vest. Women wear a head covering and usually a three-piece dress that includes a cape and an apron. The details of color and style vary from group to group. Unlike American culture, where dress is a tool of individual adornment, among the Amish it signals submission to the collective order and serves as a public symbol of group identity.

This New Order Amish home features a skylight. Refrigerators and stoves are often powered by various types of kerosene or gas—natural, propane or bottled. An inverter that pulls current from a battery powers the electric fan. Many Amish homes feature lovely wood cabinetry.

Mother, daughter, and baby. The young daughter is trying out a new pair of roller blades. Some Amish communities permit roller blades but others do not. Each church district decides its own rules.

As part of their Ordnung, most Amish groups forbid owning automobiles, tapping electricity from public utility lines, using self-propelled farm machinery, owning a television, radio, and computer, attending high school and college, joining the military, and initiating divorce. Members are expected to speak a German or Swiss dialect and to adhere to the dress standards of their group.

Members agree to obey the Ordnung at baptism. Some unbaptized youth may flirt with the world by buying a car, playing an electric guitar, or hiding a CD player in their buggy. However, after they join the church, they promptly discard the forbidden fruit.

The Church District

Families who live near each other form a local congregation called the church district. Each district has exact boundaries: creeks, roads, or township lines. About twenty to thirty-five families live in a typical district. If a family wants to join a different district, they must move to it. The church district is the social and religious hub of Amish life.

Members of each district meet for worship every other Sunday in one of their homes. The services, which rotate from home to home, often involve 150 or more children and adults. Following a three-hour worship service, members enjoy a light fellowship lunch fol-

The Twelve Largest Amish Communities

SETTLEMENT	STATE	CHURCH DISTRICTS*
Holmes County Area	Ohio	190
Lancaster County Area	Pennsylvania	150
Elkhart/LaGrange Area	Indiana	120
Geauga County Area	Ohio	85
Adams County Area	Indiana	38
Nappanee Area	Indiana	35
Arthur Area	Illinois	26
Davies County Area	Indiana	20
Mifflin County Area	Pennsylvania	20
Allen County Area	Indiana	16
Indiana County Area	Pennsylvania	15
New Wilmington Area	Pennsylvania	15

*approximate number

Amish churches have been established in some 200 communities in about twenty-five states. These are the twelve largest communities in North America based on the number of church districts.

lowed by visiting in the house or on the lawn. On their "free Sunday," members may attend services at another district or spend a quiet day at home. As districts grow, they divide. In areas with few Amish, districts may stretch across fifteen miles or more. In other districts, many families live within a mile of each other.

Each district has three types of leaders: a bishop, two ministers, and a deacon. The leaders are selected by drawing lots from nominees in the congregation. Leaders serve for life without formal training or pay. The bishop is the spiritual head of the congregation. He officiates at baptisms, weddings, communions, confessions, funerals, and members' meetings. He also interprets and enforces the Ordnung. In addition to preaching, the ministers assist with other leadership responsibilities. The deacon helps the bishop and cares for special medical or economic needs of members.

It is impossible to overstate the importance of the church district, which serves as church, club, precinct, and neighborhood all bundled together. Districts in fellowship with each other exchange ministers, support a similar Ordnung, and permit their members to intermarry. The Amish do not have church buildings, mission agencies, national religious conferences, or a central church office. Members are linked together through loose bonds of fellowship rather than by bureaucratic structures.

Religious Services and Rituals

Amish youth typically are baptized between the ages of sixteen and twenty-two. Candidates are instructed in the *Dordrecht Confession of Faith,* an old Anabaptist confession written in 1632. At baptism, youth renounce the devil and the world, confess their belief in Christ, and promise to submit to the church for the rest of their lives. Its life-long consequences make baptism a pivotal turning point. A few youth elect not to join, but the vast majority pledge their lives to the church forever. Youth who have dabbled with cars, television, popular music, and in some cases alcohol and drugs, abruptly turn their backs on these worldly things at baptism.

Holding worship services in homes reflects the simplicity and plainness of Amish life. There are no altars, candles, organs, stained glass windows, choirs, or pulpits. Slow, unison singing in German, without rhythm or instruments, unites the community together in worship. The ancient tunes are sung by memory. The words, many written by Anabaptist prisoners, are printed in a hymnbook called the *Ausbund.* An opening sermon of thirty minutes is followed by the main sermon lasting an hour or more. The leaders decide which one of them will preach during a private meeting at the beginning of the service while the congregation sings the opening hymn. The preachers speak without notes.

Fall and spring communion services rejuvenate both personal faith and the bonds of community. In a self-examination service two weeks before communion, members confess their sins publicly and reaffirm their commitment to the Ordnung. If all is well, the congregation celebrates their renewed faith in a six-hour-long communion service that includes foot washing as taught by Jesus. Unlike many Protestant services that focus on individual experience, Amish communion celebrates the unity of community. In fact, if dissension invades the church, communion may be delayed.

Like other humans, members sometimes stray into sin and deviance. Those who violate a major teaching of the Ordnung—flying in an airplane, filing a lawsuit, plowing with a tractor—will be asked to make a public confession at a members' meeting. Those who refuse or defy the authority of the church may face excommunication.

Shunning typically follows excommunication. Based on biblical teaching, shunning involves rituals that remind the wayward of their sin and seek to bring them back to fellowship. Although personal communication does not necessarily stop, members may not receive rides or goods from offenders nor sit with them during meals. Expulsion is a heavy matter because it can lead to a lifetime of estrangement from family and friends. However, those who do fall from grace

In many church districts members walk to church services that meet every other Sunday in their homes or adjacent sheds or barns. Horse-and-buggy transportation as well as walking, encourage face-to-face relationships that bond local communities together.

can always return to the fold if they are willing to confess their wrongs and mend their ways. Unbaptized persons who leave the community are not shunned.

These practices place great weight on the baptism decision for young people. Although shunning may sound harsh to modern ears, the Amish faith has two key points of integrity: adult baptism by free choice and an open back door for wayward members who want to return with a contrite heart.

Schools and Scholars

It may surprise outsiders to learn that most Amish children attended public schools before 1950. Indeed, some Amish fathers served as

Pupils in an Amish school practice for a parent's day program. The teacher is on the right, the teacher's aide is on the left. Many Amish teachers are young single women selected for their teaching ability. The children have decorated the room for this special festive occasion.

directors of rural public schools. The Amish were comfortable with small rural schools that were controlled by local parents. After World War II, many public schools required attendance until age sixteen. About the same time, many small schools closed and consolidated into large districts. Some Amish parents protested these developments because they were losing control over the nurture of their children. Moreover, they considered "book learning" and study beyond the eighth grade unnecessary for farming.

Some parents sat in prison for refusing to send their children to large public schools. For several years some states pressed charges against the Amish. Finally, in 1972, the United States Supreme Court, in a case known as *Wisconsin v. Yoder*, ruled that Amish children could end their formal schooling at eighth grade. The court concluded that "a way of life that is odd or even erratic but interferes with no rights or interests of others is not to be condemned because it is different."

Today a few Amish children still attend rural public schools, but the vast majority go to one- or two-room schools operated by Amish parents. Indeed, about 35,000 Amish youth attend some 1,300 private schools that end with eighth grade. Instruction is in English. For some "scholars," as Amish students are called, it is their first exposure to English. The teachers are typically Amish women who have not gone to high school but are graduates of Amish schools themselves. Nurtured through periodic teachers' meetings and by reading the *Blackboard Bulletin,* an Amish teacher's magazine, the teachers are largely self-trained. They are selected for their teaching ability and their embrace of Amish values.

A group of fathers, called trustees, maintains the school and hires the teacher. Parents pay tuition to support the schools. One teacher may be responsible for instructing all eight grades. In a two-room school, the grades may be divided between two teachers. A religious song and a Scripture reading may open the school day, but religion is not taught in a formal way. Reading, spelling, writing, and math are the basic subjects. Science is not taught. Most textbooks are obtained from Amish publishers.

The quality of instruction varies considerably by group and region. In some communities Amish pupils have scored very well on standardized achievement tests. However, the real test of Amish schools is not how they compare with high-tech suburban schools, but how well they prepare Amish youth for success in Amish culture. Using that standard, Amish schools appear to perform quite well. In any event, the schools play an important role in passing on Amish values, developing friendships, and limiting exposure to the outside world. The schools contribute to the vigor and vitality of Amish life.

Youth and Rumspringa

Amish youth eagerly await their sixteenth birthday, the traditional age when they begin *rumspringa,* a time of "running around." During

In many Amish communities young people begin "running around" with their peers at age sixteen. Some of them join sizable youth groups. The friends that join in a particular year are sometimes called a "buddy bunch." Activities may include sports of all kinds, hiking, or barn parties. This buddy bunch is sharing stories before a Sunday evening singing.

this time, they spend more time with their peers on weekends and often begin dating. A young man may take a girl home in his buggy after a singing or a youth group picnic. Rumspringa ends at marriage, which often occurs from nineteen to twenty-one years of age.

In the larger communities, teens typically join one of many youth groups that may claim 100 members or more. Small communities may have only one youth group. Teens that begin Rumspringa at the same time often become friends for life. In some areas those who join a youth group together are called a "buddy bunch."

Rumspringa is a moment of freedom when youth are suspended between two worlds: the control of their parents and the supervision of the church. Because they have not been baptized, they technically are not under the Ordnung. Many youth adhere to traditional Amish behavior. However, those who join more rowdy groups may experiment with worldly things—buying a car, going to movies, wearing

English clothes, buying a television or a DVD player. Parents worry about which group their child will join because the choice will influence the teen's behavior.

Youth activities may include volleyball, swimming, ice-skating, picnics, hiking at a state park, large outdoor "supper" parties, and barn parties. The most typical gatherings are singings. Groups gather in a home and sing for several hours followed by a time of fellowship and food. The "faster," more rebellious groups sometimes drive cars and attend all-night parties that feature Amish bands with electric guitars, dancing, beer, and occasionally, drugs. Although some youth engage in these activities to the dismay of their elders, many others behave in traditional ways. Even most of the wilder ones eventually stop flirting with the world and join the church.

At first glance, the rowdy youth appear as a tatter on the quilt of Amish culture. Experimenting with the world, however, can serve as

The behavior of Amish youth varies greatly in different communities and church districts. This bedroom of a progressive teenage boy shows that his interests range from tennis to hunting and archery. Without electricity, a flashlight and kerosene lamp provide lighting.

Amish courting and marriages are not arranged. A romance may begin when a young man asks to take a young woman home after a youth group singing. Young men do not grow a beard until after marriage.

a social immunization that strengthens their resistance later. A fling with worldliness gives Amish youth the impression that they have a choice regarding church membership, and indeed they do. However, all the forces of Amish life funnel them in the direction of joining the church. Knowing they have a choice, likely strengthens their willingness to obey church standards after they join. So the wild oats that are sown may, in fact, serve a useful purpose of strengthening the authority of the church in the long run.

Marriage and Family

Church and family are the primary social units of Amish society. Young people move into adulthood early and usually marry by the age of twenty-one. Daylong weddings are festive moments of celebration in Amish society. The ceremony follows a lengthy church service, held on a weekday at the home of the bride or a close relative. Several hundred guests join the festivities that often include a lunch and an evening meal.

Amish couples, on the average, have six or seven children, but in some cases, twelve or more. Most families do not use artificial birth control unless advised by a physician for health reasons; however, some do use natural methods of family planning. Some babies are born in local hospitals, but most greet the world at home or in a local birthing clinic under the supervision of a physician or certified midwife.

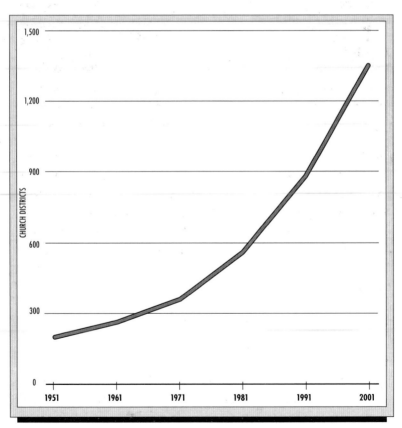

Growth of Old and New Order Church Districts, 1951–2001.

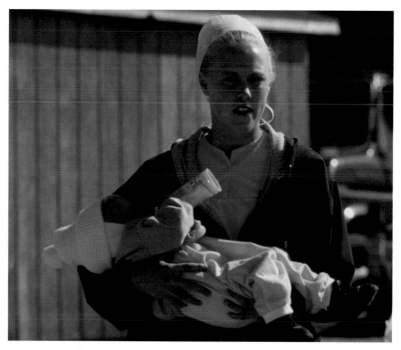

Raising a family is highly esteemed in Amish culture. Most couples begin having children soon after they are married. It is not unusual for young married women to have several children by their mid-twenties.

Amish families reflect traditional gender roles in which the man serves as the spiritual head of the home. He is responsible for its religious welfare and matters related to the church and the outside world. One husband said, "The wife is not a servant; she is the queen and the husband is the king." As in most families, gender roles in Amish marriages vary by personality. When husbands work at home, there is often considerable cross sharing of roles—women assisting in the barn or shop, and men in the garden or around the house. Wives rarely hold full-time jobs outside the family when their children are young.

Networks of extended families provide a strong sense of identity in Amish society. The typical person has more than two dozen aunts and uncles and more than seventy-five first cousins, many of whom live nearby. The family provides a dense web of social support from cradle to grave. Two or three adult women often assist a family during the arrival of a new baby. Adult sisters may gather once a month for a "sisters' day," a frolic that mixes work and fun while harvesting vegetables, cleaning house, or making quilts. Family members help each other during an emergency, a fire or flood, and of course at a death.

Because families are so large and names are similar, many people have a nickname related to a special trait or one that shows their family connection. "Horseradish Jake" may refer to someone who raises horseradish or eats a lot of it. A person named Sara may be known as "Ben's Hannah's Sara," referring to her mother and grandfather. The large Amish community near Lancaster, Pennsylvania, has over 100 people named Mary Stoltzfus and at least ninety Katie Stoltzfuses.

The Amish do not have retirement homes. The elderly normally live in an apartment in a home of one of their children or in a *Grossdawdy Haus,* a small adjacent house. Some grandparents have more

Amish communities are skilled at cooking for large social gatherings such as weddings and benefit auctions. Men and women often work closely together when preparing and serving food for such occasions.

than eighty grandchildren and 200 great-grandchildren. Esteemed for their wisdom, the elderly find meaning and dignity as they assist their adult children. Surrounded by droves of grandchildren, they pass on the wisdom, joys, and secrets of Amish life to the rising generation.

Food and Health

Most Amish families have bountiful gardens. Nevertheless, many staples—sugar, flour, cereal, coffee, yogurt, ice cream, pretzels, and chips—are purchased at retail stores. Some families also rely on store-bought bread, instant pudding, instant drink mixes, commer-

Amish homes typically do not have electricity. This treadle sewing machine is in a traditional Amish home. Some sewing machines are operated by air power or 12-volt current from a battery. Sometimes small appliances are also operated by air power or batteries.

cial snack foods, and canned soups. Bulk quantities of store-bought canned fruits, cereals, and noodles are popular in many communities. One woman noted that, "Gardens are hardly worth the effort when you can buy canned fruits and vegetables in bulk so cheap." Many families butcher their own beef and pork. Non-farmers may arrange to receive fresh meat from families or friends who butcher. Most Amish families still rely much more on gardens and home-preserved foods than their English neighbors.

The food prepared by Amish cooks varies by the region of the country. In Eastern Pennsylvania, Amish families enjoy regional specialties such as shoofly pie, sauerkraut, and scrapple (ground pork and beef combined with flour and cornmeal). Regardless of the regional fare, Amish foods are preserved and prepared in volume to feed large families and sizable numbers of visitors. It is not uncommon for a family to can 150 quarts of applesauce, 100 quarts of peaches, and similar amounts of pears, grape juice, or other local fruits. Some families can as many as fifty quarts of tomato sauce for making homemade pizza. A family may bake three dozen pies for the fellowship meal following the church service at their home. A twelve-year-old girl may carry the weekly responsibility for baking a dozen loaves of bread for her family. Other families buy their bread at the store. Because Amish homes do not have electricity, canning is the customary means of preserving food. Some families rent lockers at local stores or keep a deep freezer at the home of an English neighbor.

The quality of healthcare varies considerably from community to community. Members of more isolated, conservative groups may only see a doctor for an extreme emergency—a broken leg or a heart attack. More progressive families consult a family doctor on a regular basis. Some families use state-of-the-art medical technology for heart surgery or even organ transplants.

In general, Amish families prefer natural treatments to chemical ones. An herbal tea is often preferred over an aspirin. Many people visit a chiropractor on a regular basis for various treatments. In more conservative families, high tech fixes are only sought, if at all, after natural remedies fail. Amish patients frequently seek relief through alternative, homeopathic treatments and from non-traditional practitioners. Some patients travel to unlicensed clinics in Mexico for treatment of cancer or other ailments. Natural remedies are viewed by many Amish as being closer to God's order in nature and therefore more trustworthy than complicated scientific interventions.

Stewards of the Soil

Ever since religious persecution pushed them into rural areas in Europe, the Amish have been tillers of the soil—and good ones. Their ties to the land have supported their common life and served as a cradle for the nurture of their children. Almost without exception, Amish parents will say the farm is the best place to raise children. It is a social seedbed where children learn the virtues of responsibility, hard work, and teamwork. "Good soil," said one leader, "makes a strong church where we can live together, worship together, and work together." On the farm—tilling the soil, cultivating crops, and caring for animals—one is closer to nature and to God.

With large families, Amish farming has always been a family affair. Church leaders have resisted large-scale mechanized farming that would steal work from children and erode family involvement. Using horse-drawn equipment is one way of resisting large, corporate style farming. With a few exceptions, most farms are small family operations that use horses to pull machinery in the fields. Many farms have a tractor at the barn for high power needs such as blowing silage to the top of silos, grinding grain, or pumping liquid manure.

For many years, Amish farms were small, diversified operations with a dozen cows, some chickens, and a few beef cattle. Although many continue this tradition, other farms have become more specialized with dairy, and in some cases, with chickens or hogs. Specialized farms tend to be more mechanized, but always less so than their English neighbors. Farmers with more than twenty cows typically use

Farm technology varies greatly among different Amish subgroups. More traditional groups use old-fashioned hay loaders and transport loose hay on wagons into their barns as in the top photo. More progressive groups use state-of-the-art hay balers adapted for horses.

mechanical milkers and bulk cooling tanks. The more traditional farmers milk by hand and ship their milk in old-fashioned cans to cheese plants at a lower price. Economic pressures have encouraged more mechanization in many Amish communities.

Despite popular myths, many Amish farmers do not practice organic farming. Most of them use insecticides, herbicides, and chemical fertilizers. There is a growing trend toward small specialty operations that produce vegetables, herbs, greenhouse plants, and flowers. Some of these operations are fully organic to target special urban markets. A growing number of farmers specialize in raising exotic game animals: buffalo, llamas, deer, quail, or pheasants. Others raise puppies for pet stores.

Economic pressures have encouraged many families to seek non-farm employment, but many of them continue to blend off-farm work with sideline farming that involves their children. The most conservative groups have stubbornly resisted non-farm work and continue to cling to small family farms with little mechanization. Most families, regardless of their work, sing the virtues of farm life for raising children in the Amish faith.

Business

Despite their love of farming, the majority of Amish in many settlements have abandoned their plows. In some of the larger communities, the number of farmers dips below 15 percent. More isolated communities in some areas still claim over 75 percent on the farm. The shift to non-farm work is the biggest change in Amish society in the last century. Despite their growing involvement in business and commerce, the Amish remain a distinctly rural people, living along country roads and on the margins of small villages. Many families combine off-farm work with hobby farming. Three types of non-farm work flourish: small shops, construction work, and employment in English factories.

This Amish manufacturing shop makes sizable quantities of farm implements such as these plows for both Amish and non-Amish farmers and distributes the equipment in many states and provinces.

Hundreds of small Amish-owned industries have sprung up in many communities in recent years. Most of these are small family businesses with less than ten employees. The bulk of them produce wood products—household and outdoor furniture, gazebos, small barns, lawn ornaments, doghouses, and mailboxes—to name but a few of the hundreds. Other shops specialize in fabricating metal. Some of these build farm machinery, but others hold contracts with outside English vendors and large national chains such as Wal-Mart. Amish retail stores that sell hardware, dry goods, and food are also on the rise. With low overhead and ample family labor, the small home-based shops are very productive and profitable. Annual sales in the larger businesses may exceed five million dollars.

Construction work also provides employment for many Amish men. In some areas dozens of construction crews travel considerable distances to build homes and industrial buildings for non-Amish people. Amish-owned construction companies often hire non-Amish employees who also drive the crews to job sites. Church rules governing the use of electrical tools are often relaxed at away-from-home construction sites. The more conservative Amish groups discourage construction work because it increases exposure to technology and interaction with the outside world.

In some communities, the majority of Amish men work in factories owned by English, located in rural areas. In northern Indiana, many Amish work in factories that build recreational vehicles. Several hundred Amish may work in a factory, creating in effect, a small Amish world in the midst of a high-tech operation. Fringe benefits, like medical insurance and social security that come with English factory employment, can tempt members not to rely on the church for mutual aid.

Many Amish shops and some homes have a diesel engine as their main source of power. The diesel engines power hydraulic pumps, air pumps, and generators that provide power for various types of shop, farm, and home machinery. Water in many homes and farms is pumped by air pressure. Other more traditional settlements have homes which still use windmills or gasoline engines to pump water.

Some Amish businesses are owned and operated by women. A woman entrepreneur developed this dried flower shop from which she distributes her products around the world. A propane lantern provides light.

The growth of non-farm employment has brought new wealth to many Amish communities. Some elders worry that the new jobs bring too much "easy money and ready cash in pockets" and in time, will erode a work ethic built on generations of farming. Many Amish communities prefer home-based shops to "lunch pail jobs" where fathers work away from home. "What we're trying to do," said one young shop owner, "is to keep the family together."

The Puzzles of Technology

Many people mistakenly think the Amish reject technology. It is more accurate to say that they use technology selectively. Televisions, radios, and computers are rejected out right, but many other

Because Amish businesses do not use electricity from public utility lines, many of them power large machinery with air or hydraulic power from a diesel. Mechanics remove the electric motors from machines and replace them with air or hydraulic motors. This planer, run by hydraulic, trims wood in an Amish furniture shop.

types of technology are used selectively or modified to fit Amish purposes. Amish mechanics also create new machines to fit their cultural needs. Moreover, much state-of-the-art technology, like gas grills, shop tools, camping equipment, and some farm equipment, is readily bought from non-Amish vendors.

Why do the Amish fear technology? If left untamed, they worry that technology will harm their community by disrupting trustworthy traditions and bringing foreign values through mass media. They strike a distinction between sinfulness and worldliness. Technology is not considered evil in itself; "It's what it will do to the next generation," said one bishop. A car is not seen as immoral, but as a harmful tool that would pull the community apart.

The puzzles of Amish technology are perplexing to outsiders. Why would God frown on a telephone? What sense does it make to keep a tractor at the barn but not take it to the field? Is it not inconsistent, if not outright hypocritical, to hire rides in cars but refuse to own them? And what could be the difference between 12-volt electric from batteries and 110-volt currents from public utility lines? These distinctions may look silly to an outsider, but within the context of Amish history, they are important cultural compromises that help to slow the pace of social change. Such adaptations reflect the struggles of Amish communities to balance tradition and change without being swallowed up by modern technology.

An Amish businessman uses his cell phone to make some out of state contacts. Most Amish communities oppose the installation of private phones in their houses. Cell phones have created controversies in some Amish communities. More traditional communities do not permit their members to use phones except for an emergency, in which case they use public phones or one in the home of an English neighbor.

Many Amish groups permit tractors to be used at the barn for high power needs but not in the field to pull machinery. Leaders worry that using tractors for fieldwork will lead to full-scale mechanization and destroy the family farm. Steel wheels are often preferred because air filled tires would encourage using tractors on the road for shopping and might, in time, lead to a car. Horse-and-buggy transportation keeps the community anchored on a local geographical base. Cars would bring greater mobility that would pull the community apart. Although they prohibit owning motor vehicles, many Amish groups permit members to hire "taxis" driven by English neighbors to travel to distant weddings or funerals and to visit kin in far-flung settlements. Many Amish businessowners hire vans and trucks on a daily basis for their business needs.

Most Amish groups forbid electricity from public utility lines. "It's not the electricity that is so bad," said one member, "it's all the things we don't need that would come with it." Television, computers, radio, and all sorts of modern conveniences might follow on the coattails of electricity. Electricity from batteries is more local, controllable, and independent from the outside world. Batteries are used to power many things: lights on buggies, calculators, fans, flashlights, cash registers, copy machines, and typewriters. Solar energy is sometimes used to charge batteries, operate electric fences, or power some household appliances.

Amish shops typically have a diesel engine for power. Air and hydraulic (oil) pumps driven by a gas or diesel engine operate saws, grinders, sanders, lathes, and metal presses. The electric motors on new equipment are replaced with air or hydraulic motors. Many shop owners claim that air or hydraulic power is, in fact, more efficient than electric. Some of the more conservative groups only use tools that are powered by belts from a gasoline or diesel engine. Each local community decides where to draw the line.

The Amish seek to master technology rather than becoming its slave. They try to tame technology—hoping to prevent it from harming family and community life.

Community Rhythms

A strong sense of community regulates the rhythms of Amish life. Face to face conversation in homes, lawns, shops, and barns provides the social glue of Amish society. Without big organizations, Amish life thrives in a thicket of personal relationships that mix neighborhood, family, church, work, and leisure together. Despite many communal regulations, each individual is afforded respect and dignity. Church, family, and community are woven together in a single fabric, very different from the sharp separation of roles in mainstream society.

One of the tenets of Amish faith is care and concern for fellow members of the church. Members reach out to those in need and know that they too will receive care as needs arise. Following a flood or fire, the Amish community rallies quickly to clean up the debris and construct a new building. The traditional Amish barn raising illustrates the power and meaning of community in practical ways as

Amish work frolics often blend work, fellowship, and fun. Amish and Mennonite women gather here in a home for a quilting frolic.

hundreds of people converge to erect a new structure in a day. Some-times, Amish people also travel outside their community to assist English families that are victims of a tornado, hurricane, or other natural disaster.

The habits of mutual aid stretch beyond floods and fires. Because they do not have commercial insurance, many Amish communities have an informal aid plan to help members with large hospital bills. Faced with large bills or other exceptional needs, local congregations take a special offering, collected by the deacon in a door to door visit. A public benefit auction or bake sale may also be used to raise funds for special needs. An injured farmer will usually find his crops harvested by a bevy of neighbors with horse-drawn implements.

Many rhythms of community go beyond disaster and medical needs. Parents gather to clean up local schools in preparation for the new academic year. Families who are moving can expect dozens of

From birth to death the Amish are surrounded by community. Members of a church district prepare a grave for a burial. Reflecting the equality of community, Amish gravestones are typically the same size and modest in their simplicity. Smaller stones signal the graves of children.

Corner ball is a favorite game in some communities. The four players on the outside circle try to hit the player from the opposing team in the center. This game is being played in a barnyard during an auction.

hands to carry furniture. Extended family members and neighbors will gather in a work frolic to paint a house for newlyweds. Several adult siblings may meet monthly in a frolic for sewing, house cleaning, shelling peas, or canning tomatoes. And of course, there are always quilting parties to attend. In addition to work, the frequent visiting, which one member called "the national sport" of Amish life, bonds the community together.

Recreation and Leisure

Recreation in Amish life often focuses on local activities involving nature. Without cars and with many chores, families are tied to the local community. Sledding, skating, swimming, fishing, and hunting provide breaks from the routines of work. Informal games of soft-

Many Amish enjoy outdoor sports such as hunting, fishing, and skating. This young man is unloading his boat for a fishing trip. Although some communities permit outboard motors for fishing, speedboats for water skiing are generally discouraged for members.

ball, corner ball, and volleyball have been longtime favorites in many Amish communities. Some children play with homemade toys and create their own games. Others use bright colored plastic toys, tricycles, and Big Wheels.

Historically, endless farm chores underscored the importance of work. Families had little time for leisure. Indeed, pleasure and amusement were considered not only a waste of time, but outright evil. Idleness, viewed as the devil's workshop, would lead to mischief or other vices. These attitudes still prevail in the more conservative communities, but among the non-farm Amish, recreational practices are changing.

Families involved in business or factory work are finding more time for recreation. "We are more of a leisure people now," said one businessman. Another shop owner said "We're business people now, not just backwoods farmers, and sometimes we just need to get away." Several couples may travel together in a hired van to visit friends and relatives in other, out-of-state communities. Along the way, they may visit historic sites or stop at a state or national park. Large groups sometimes charter a bus to a historic village, a zoo, or a natural site as well. Family reunions and picnics are also popular times for visiting and relaxing.

Groups of men sometimes rent a hunting cabin for several days or charter a boat to go deep sea fishing in the Atlantic or fishing on one of the Great Lakes, depending on where they live. Archery is popular in some areas. Another favorite hobby is bird watching. Adults who enjoy birding sometimes travel across the country to popular migration sites. Some young men go big game hunting in the Rocky Mountains for a week equipped with guides and state-of-the-art guns and supplies. Young people sometimes ski on water or snow depending on where they live.

Recreation and travel is on the rise among more progressive families. Nevertheless, Amish leisure for the most part is not commercialized and remains entrenched in nature. Also, it is almost always community oriented, revolving around family and friends.

Softball and volleyball are popular forms of recreation in many Amish communities. Volleyball nets are often stretched between two carriages.

Government and Outside Ties

Contrary to public misperception, the Amish do pay taxes. They pay state and federal income taxes, sales and real estate taxes, and public school taxes. In fact, they pay school taxes twice because they also support their own private schools. They are exempt from paying social security taxes because they consider social security a form of insurance. The Amish believe that the Bible instructs them to care for the elderly and assist members who have special needs. To rely on commercial or government insurance would mock their faith that God will care for them through the church.

Following a long struggle that involved fines and imprisonment, the U.S. Congress exempted the Amish from the Social Security system in 1966. Under this legislation they do not pay into or receive Social Security, Medicaid, or Medicare payments. However, English employers of Amish must pay Social Security for their Amish employees. Some states have also exempted Amish businesses from paying Worker's Compensation taxes for job-related injuries because the Amish consider that an insurance as well.

In some areas Amish people work in businesses and factories owned by non-Amish. This is the Ohio corporate headquarters of a garage door business that employs Amish people in its manufacturing plants.

The Amish are taught to respect and pray for governing authorities according to biblical admonitions. However, when caught in a conflict between their conscience and civic law, the Amish recite the Scripture that they should "obey God rather than man." The intense persecution in Europe solidified their strong belief in the separation of church and state. The Amish are pacifists and refuse to enter the armed forces. They generally avoid politics, holding office, and political activism. They are, however, permitted to vote. The rate of voting is typically low unless a local issue is on the ballot.

In recent years, numerous conflicts have pitted the Amish against the growing power of the state to regulate public behavior. The points of friction included military service, education, social security, health care, property zoning, child labor, and the use of slow moving vehicle signs. To cope with the growing regulations that pricked their conscience, the Amish formed a National Steering Committee with representatives in various states to work with public legislators when issues arise. All things considered, the Amish have fared rather well in a political system that respects and protects their freedom of religious expression.

The Amish generally do not join public organizations or service clubs in the local community. Some of them, however, are members of local volunteer fire companies and emergency medical units. Although they do not develop intimate relationships with outsiders or marry them, they are usually good neighbors who enjoy many friendships with English neighbors and friends.

———————◆—————

Amish Wisdom

The Amish community is not perfect. Like other humans, Amish hearts sometimes swell with greed, jealousy, and anger. Parents worry about their children and some youth rebel as in other societies. Although divorce is forbidden, marriages sometimes sour. Occasionally, some leaders abuse their power. There are also sporadic reports

Amish people from several states travel to Sarasota, Florida, each winter to enjoy the sun. Many of them live in cottages in a small village called Pinecraft. They spend this vacation time visiting, playing shuffleboard, cruising about in large tricycles, and visiting friends.

of sexual and physical abuse in families. Disagreements sometimes debilitate congregational life and force communion to be postponed until harmony is restored. "We are not perfect," said one Amish man. "We have our own set of problems."

Despite the blemishes, the Amish have developed a remarkable society. With little government aid or scientific assistance, they provide care and dignity for their members. Apart from occasional arrests for alcohol or drug abuse among their youth, the Amish have avoided many of the blights of modern life. They have virtually no homeless, no unemployed, no one living on government subsidies, few in prison, few divorces, and few cases of serious abuse. Thus, all things considered, they have created a rather humane society without high school education, professional training, or high tech accessories.

There are many things we can learn from our Amish neighbors, but several shreds of wisdom are noteworthy. First, their respect for tradition underscores the importance of communal wisdom. Rather than turn to individual intellect and personal experience for authority, the Amish turn to the historical wisdom stored in their cultural reservoir. The combined wisdom of the community, they believe, is more reliable than the rational speculations of even a well-trained individual.

Second, they consider the welfare of the church community to be more important than individual freedom. Yielding selfish desires to the will of the church, they believe, in the long run brings deep meaning and purpose to life. In their eyes, pride and individualism are destructive. Humility, self-denial, and obedience to the community bring peace and joy.

Third, the Amish have learned the importance of taming technology so that it serves, rather than controls their community. Like few other communities, they have had the courage and tenacity to tackle the powerful forces of technology in order to preserve their traditional way of life. In short, community well-being supercedes individual freedom to use technology.

Fourth, apart from large families, the Amish emphasize the importance of small-scale, informal social relations. "Bigness ruins everything," said one Amish carpenter. Schools are small, church districts are limited by the size of homes, and the church restrains the size of businesses. Intimate, face-to-face relationships add dignity and respect to human interaction.

The Amish have learned to live with limits. Indeed, they would argue that setting and respecting limits on almost everything is one of the foundations of wisdom. Limits, for the Amish, are a necessary requirement for human happiness. Without limits, individuals become arrogant, conceited, and self-destructive. And although restraints may appear to stifle individual freedom at first, they may in fact, grant greater dignity and security to the individual than the endless choices and rotating options of modern life. A respect for limits builds community, brings belonging, and shapes identity—three important keys to human satisfaction and happiness.

In some ways, the Amish trouble us, even torment us. We worry that without modern technology, higher education, the latest fashions, and unfettered freedom, they might, in fact, be just as happy, if not happier than the rest of us. And so the Amish enchant and trouble us at the same time. They prod us to reflect on the sources of meaning and purpose, on the roots of human happiness.

Additional Resources

Granick, Eve Wheatcroft. *The Amish Quilt.* Intercourse, Pa.: Good Books, 1989.

Kraybill, Donald B. *The Riddle of Amish Culture.* Rev. ed. Baltimore: Johns Hopkins University Press, 2001.

Kraybill, Donald B., ed. *The Amish and The State.* Rev. ed. Baltimore: Johns Hopkins University Press, 2003.

Kraybill, Donald B. and Carl Desportes Bowman. *On the Backroad to Heaven: Old Order Hutterites, Mennonites, Amish and Brethren.* Baltimore: Johns Hopkins University Press, 2001.

Kraybill, Donald B. and Steven M. Nolt. *Amish Enterprise: From Plows to Profits.* Rev. ed. Baltimore: Johns Hopkins University Press, 2003.

Kraybill, Donald B., and C. Nelson Hostetter. *Anabaptist World USA.* Scottdale, Pa.: Herald Press, 2001.

Miller, Bob and Sue, eds. *Amish Country Cookbook.* Vol. 1–3. Nappanee, Ind.: Evangel Publishing House, 2001.

Nolt, Steven M. *A History of the Amish.* Rev. ed. Intercourse, Pa.: Good Books, 2003.

Scott, Stephen M. *Plain Buggies: Amish, Mennonite and Brethren Horse-drawn Transportation.* Rev. ed. Intercourse, Pa.: Good Books, 1998.

——- *Why Do They Dress That Way?* Rev. ed. Intercourse, Pa.: Good Books, 1997.

——- *The Amish Wedding and Other Special Occasions of the Old Order Communities.* Intercourse, Pa.: Good Books, 1988.

Stoltzfus, Louise. *Amish Women: Lives and Stories.* Intercourse, Pa.: Good Books, 1994.

Umble, Diane Zimmerman. *Holding the Line: The Telephone in Old Order Mennonite and Amish Life.* Baltimore: John Hopkins University Press, 1996.

Weaver-Zercher, David. *The Amish in the American Imagination.* Baltimore: John Hopkins University Press, 2001.